Pendennis Castle and St Mawes Castle

Paul Pattison

Introduction

Situated near the western tip of England, for over 400 years the Cornish fortresses of Pendennis and St Mawes have guarded the entrance to Carrick Roads, a vast anchorage that fostered the port of Falmouth. In the 17th century Falmouth developed as an important port, as the first safe landfall for ships crossing the Atlantic or heading from the Mediterranean into the English Channel.

The importance of Carrick Roads lay in the potential security it offered to the nation's enemies as a base for invasion: a toehold in England. Pendennis and St Mawes Castles were built in the 1540s during a national defence programme under Henry VIII. Both were artillery forts designed to prevent hostile warships entering Carrick Roads. Between 1597 and 1600, under threat of Spanish invasion, Pendennis was given the bastioned defences visible today. These were tested in 1646 when desperate troops, loyal to King Charles I, were starved into surrender by victorious parliamentary forces during the Civil War.

The castles saw little action in the 18th century, but became important again between 1807 and 1813, when Falmouth acted as a re-supply base for the British Army at war in Spain and Portugal. Improvements during Victorian times strengthened the defences, notably the Grand Sea Battery at St Mawes, and by 1900 Falmouth had become a complex coastal fortress with powerful new weapons united in a sophisticated defence plan controlled centrally from Pendennis. Gun positions of this period can be seen at One-Gun Battery and Half-Moon Battery at Pendennis.

Throughout the First and Second World Wars Falmouth was a defended port with formidable fortifications. On 6 June 1944, during the greatest seaborne invasion in history, troops embarked from Falmouth under the cover of the guns of Pendennis, St Mawes and St Anthony Head – the last major episode in a military history that ended when the Army left in 1956.

Below: A bugler and companion at Pendennis during the First World War

Facing page: The elegant St Mawes Castle, overlooking the entrance to Carrick Roads

Tour of Pendennis Castle

**FOLLOWING
THE TOUR**

*This tour divides into two
parts. The first part of the
tour takes the visitor around
the main parts of the fortress
with its spectacular views of
the Cornish coastline. The
second part of the tour takes
in Little Dennis blockhouse
and Crab Quay on Pendennis
Point. These can be reached
by car or on foot from the
site car park. The numbers
beside the headings highlight
the key points on the tour
and correspond with the
small numbered plans in
the margins.*

Dominating a high, rocky headland thrust out into the open sea, the great fortress of Pendennis protected the entrance to the river Fal and its vast deep estuary, Carrick Roads, for over 400 years. A walk around the inside of the fort reveals the geometric perfection of the Elizabethan ramparts, which were completed in 1600 and still define the perimeter. A host of guns and emplacements bristle from the ramparts, illustrating the ever-changing technology of artillery warfare, which is explored further in the Discovery Centre and exhibition.

At the heart of the fortress, gracing the highest point, is Pendennis Castle itself, Henry VIII's elegant circular gun tower of the 1540s, where the sounds and smells of the guns are recreated. Located nearby are the Battery Observation Post and war shelter, from which the fortress guns were controlled and where gunners awaited the call to action during the two world wars of the 20th century. The huge guns of the Second World War can be reached through a tunnel under the ramparts to Half-Moon Battery.

◻ GATEHOUSE AND GUARD BARRACKS

On either side of the entrance are the steep, grassy ramparts of the Elizabethan fortress. The entrance was originally a simple arched passage through the rampart, approached across a wooden bridge; the final span was a drawbridge operated by a counterbalance mechanism from the passage. The original bridge and counterbalance have gone, but at the inner end of the passage are two arched alcoves, one of which contains the mechanism for a later drawbridge, which went out of use in about 1849 when the present solid bridge was made. The gatehouse over the passage, with its imposing classical front, was added in about 1700.

The passage emerges between the guard barracks. They are solid structures of dressed granite, also built in about 1700, and among the earliest surviving barracks in Britain. The functions of the southern block have varied, including use as a hospital, a schoolroom and a carpenter's workshop. The northern block always housed the guard and was modernised in the early 20th century to include cells for unruly soldiers. Today, this block is dressed as a guard room of the First World War, when its cells housed miscreant soldiers and, occasionally, civilians suspected (often in error) of spying for the enemy.

◻ STOREHOUSE

This fine brick store, its walls originally covered with slates, was built between 1793 and 1811 as one of three storehouses at Pendennis that contained supplies for British troops fighting against Napoleon's army in Spain and Portugal. By 1866 it had been converted into a hospital, with a kitchen and scullery, and in the early 20th century

Left: The gatehouse, reached by a bridge that spans a dry ditch, guards the main entrance to Pendennis
Below: 'Went the day well?' Detail of a Second World War cartoon by George Butterworth
Bottom: Inside Pendennis, showing (left to right), the sergeants' mess, guard barracks, storehouse and RGA barracks with Falmouth beyond
Facing page: Aerial view of Pendennis headland

it became a canteen and billiard room, as conditions for soldiers were improved. Today there is a shop on the ground floor, while the upper floor houses a display of cartoons by George Butterworth (1905–88), the foremost political cartoonist of the Second World War, whose work appeared frequently in national newspapers of the time.

◻ ROYAL GARRISON ARTILLERY BARRACKS

Erected between 1900 and 1902, this imposing building was a barracks and headquarters for the 105th Regiment of the Royal Garrison Artillery (RGA). It was divided into rooms to hold 11 or 12 private soldiers in each, with shared washing areas, while corporals and sergeants had single rooms. Within the central tower is a huge 90,000-litre (20,000-gallon) water tank, while a clock, so important for the strict military routine, faces the parade ground. The 140 regular soldiers of the

Right: The parade ground during the First World War, with temporary barracks and facilities huts. The building on the left was probably the YMCA (its interior at the time is shown on page 47)
Below: The guard room office, decorated and equipped as it may have been during the First World War

RGA lived here between 1902 and 1911, after which they were replaced by volunteers of the Territorial Force (now the TA). The exhibition on the first floor, 'Fortress Falmouth and the First World War', reveals the important role played by Pendennis and Falmouth between 1914 and 1918. A cookhouse, baths and latrines behind the barracks have since been demolished. Of the same period as the barracks are bungalows to the north and south. These were once used as a storehouse for the Army Service Corps (1904) and a Sergeants' Mess (1911). Both are now holiday cottages.

4 PARADE GROUND

The large space of the fort interior was not always so open. It has changed as buildings came and went, whether temporary wooden structures or permanent barracks and stores. There was even a windmill during the Civil War (1642–51). In the First World War barrack huts of corrugated iron covered the whole area, and in the Second World War temporary huts were also used.

It is possible to walk around most of the Elizabethan ramparts; five of the original six bastions are intact and are presented with artillery pieces from various periods of the fortress's history.

5 EAST BASTION

Bastions first appeared in Italy in about 1500 in response to the power of gunpowder artillery, which could easily destroy the high walls and towers of medieval castles. Bastions were low platforms for artillery that presented a difficult target for enemy guns. Angle bastions, like those at Pendennis, had two 'faces' for heavy guns to fire at distant targets and two 'flanks' for smaller guns to fire alongside the ramparts and adjacent bastions. In this way each bastion supported its neighbour with interlocking fire against a siege or assault.

East Bastion originally had four guns that fired through embrasures in the parapet, but was modified on several occasions. Sections of the older stone parapets survive, but the concrete emplacements were inserted in 1902 for two 12-pounder quick-firing (QF) guns to protect Carrick Roads from torpedo boats.

Steps lead to underground magazines and a shelter for the gunners. After 1905 the guns were used only for training, until 1941, when the magazines were converted into a Battery Plotting Room for Falmouth Fire Command. Information was relayed to this room from observation posts and radar stations, and converted into accurate target locations. Targets were then allocated to individual guns by the Fire Commander.

6 NINE-GUN BATTERY

Extensive alterations to the Elizabethan ramparts in the 1730s included the creation of Nine-Gun Battery, overlooking Carrick Roads and armed with nine muzzle-loading guns. The guns on display, of late 18th- and early 19th-century date, stand on original stone platforms and look through original embrasures.

7 FIELD TRAIN SHED

This shed is the remaining half of an original structure, built in 1805, for a field train of mobile guns, wagons, gun carriages, wheels and baggage, stored until needed in action. It was a low building with roof windows and doors in each gable, through which equipment was driven in or out along a roadway, on either side of which was room for storage. Today it houses the Discovery Centre – a thematic and hands-on look at coastal defence.

8 ONE-GUN BATTERY

In the 1890s, the first breech-loading (BL) guns were installed in coastal defences nationwide. These guns were easier and quicker to operate than earlier muzzle-loaders. In 1895 Pendennis received three 6-inch BL guns, one emplaced here in Bell Bastion with an adjacent underground magazine. On firing, the gun barrel recoiled on pivoting steel arms, 'disappearing' into the gun pit through a steel shield under which the gunners reloaded in safety. The spare energy of the recoil was stored as pressure by hydro-pneumatic cylinders with pistons attached to the arms. Releasing that pressure caused the barrel to return smoothly to the firing position.

Although the idea of a gun that disappeared from the view of enemy ships at sea was good,

the mounting was prone to breakdown. It was replaced by another type that controlled recoil along the line of the barrel, which was quicker to operate. The disappearing gun in One-Gun Battery was obsolete by 1905 and removed in 1913. The 6-inch barrel on display is on a fixed mounting which allows it to be seen close to the original firing position. On the edge of the battery, the small rectangular concrete building may be of First World War date, though it probably remained in use through the Second World War. It was possibly an observation position from which watch was kept for enemy ships, submarines and airships. From 1925 the job of lookout for aircraft became the responsibility of a special unit called the Royal Observer Corps.

Left: The sunken magazine (foreground) and deep gun pit (centre) of One-Gun Battery

Below: The largest warships of the 18th century had as many as 100 guns, but small groups of guns on shore, as here at Nine-Gun Battery, had the advantage of firm ground, rather than rolling sea

9 THE CASTLE

Pendennis Castle was part of a national building programme of coastal artillery forts, begun in 1539 by Henry VIII in response to the threat of invasion by French and Spanish forces. Henry's fort has four main elements: a guardhouse, a forebuilding, a central round tower and a surrounding gun platform (the 'chemise').

Although designed as a gun fort, from the middle of the 17th century the castle was used as accommodation, offices, an officers' mess and storage. During the Second World War it became the headquarters of Falmouth Fire Command.

The approach is through an arch in the rear wall of the Tudor guardhouse, most of which was taken down in 1902 and replaced by another building, itself demolished in 1921. Beyond it, a stone bridge built in 1902 to replace an earlier wooden one crosses the ditch to the forebuilding entrance.

The forebuilding was added to the tower and chemise in the second half of the 16th century, replacing an original building with an entrance between square towers.

Its exterior has restrained touches of ornamentation, with a fine oriel window and gargoyles projecting from a cordon below the parapet. The entrance has an empty recess above it, perhaps for the governor's coat of arms, and above that an elaborate carving of the Tudor royal arms. Columns at the end of the bridge supported a horizontal wooden beam that guided the chains of a separate drawbridge through slots above the entrance to a portcullis in a room behind. The drawbridge and the portcullis were carefully counterbalanced for easy operation from inside.

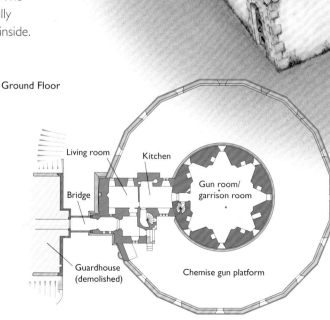

FLOOR PLANS OF PENDENNIS CASTLE

Basement

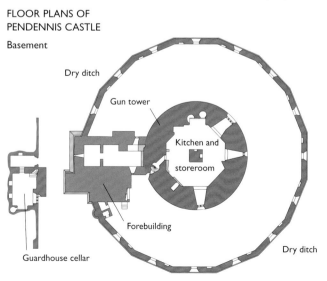

Dry ditch

Gun tower

Kitchen and storeroom

Forebuilding

Guardhouse cellar

Dry ditch

Ground Floor

Living room

Kitchen

Bridge

Gun room/ garrison room

Guardhouse (demolished)

Chemise gun platform

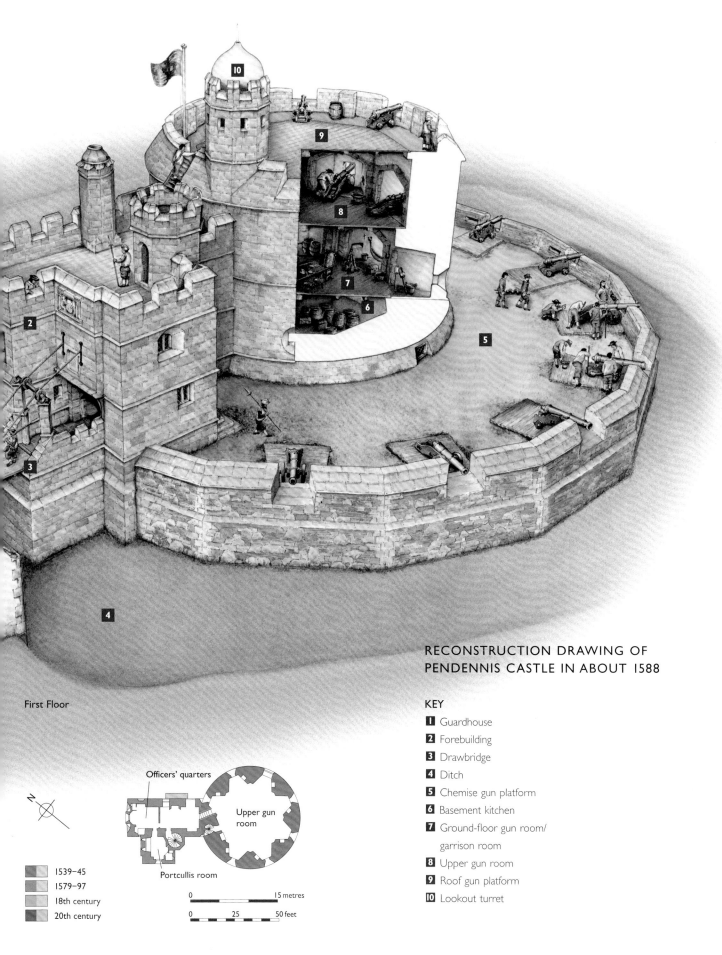

RECONSTRUCTION DRAWING OF
PENDENNIS CASTLE IN ABOUT 1588

KEY

1 Guardhouse
2 Forebuilding
3 Drawbridge
4 Ditch
5 Chemise gun platform
6 Basement kitchen
7 Ground-floor gun room/
  garrison room
8 Upper gun room
9 Roof gun platform
10 Lookout turret

First Floor

Officers' quarters

Upper gun
room

Portcullis room

1539–45
1579–97
18th century
20th century

0 ――――――― 15 metres
0 ――― 25 ――― 50 feet

Roof

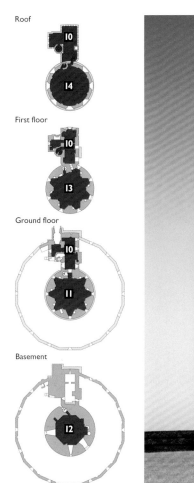

First floor

Ground floor

Basement

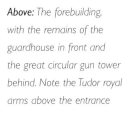

Above: The forebuilding, with the remains of the guardhouse in front and the great circular gun tower behind. Note the Tudor royal arms above the entrance

10 Forebuilding

This housed the apartments of the commanding officer, who in Tudor times was one of the Killigrew family (see the feature box on page 33). It has two floors of three rooms each and a defensible roof. Once inside the lobby, a door leads straight onto the chemise and another led (east) into a pair of rooms. The left-hand (northern) of the pair may have been another guardroom and contains an unusual oval window. In the 18th century it was a living room for the commanding officer. The right-hand (southern) room, with its large fireplace and baking oven, served as his kitchen, but was also the route into the gun tower and, via a spiral stair, to the first floor and roof.

The three first-floor rooms are now simply furnished to reflect their use by officers, the first room as an 18th-century dining room and the second as a bedroom with its oriel window and private latrine. The third room contains the portcullis over the main entrance. The roof is crenellated for defence by handguns.

11 Gun Tower – Ground-floor Gun Room

From the forebuilding, the tower entrance was guarded by doors at both ends of the wall thickness. The inner doors were defended by a circular hole cut through the wall at an angle, through which a handgun could be fired.

The large octagonal room was originally designed as a gun floor, like that reconstructed in the upper gun room. During construction, the design of the castle was adapted and the external chemise, which took over the role of gun floor, was built. This room became the living area for the garrison, although the features of the room reflect its original purpose.

Seven alcoves in the walls were for heavy guns on wheeled wooden carriages, which fired through circular embrasures. Each one has a smoke vent in its vault, an alcove in one side wall for supplies of shot and powder, and square slots in the side walls for timbers to secure shutters when the guns were not in use. A small latrine is built into the side of one alcove. By 1715 the room was partitioned with a central passage and six rooms. At that time these were empty, but they had been used to store gunpowder.

⓬ Gun Tower – Basement Kitchen

A spiral stair in the tower wall leads to the basement, which has a flagstone floor and a ceiling supported by a central pier. Now one large space, it was originally partitioned as a kitchen, cellar and larder for the Tudor garrison. The large fireplace was for cooking, with a baking oven on either side.

A recess to the left of the fire contained a cistern for rainwater brought by lead pipes from the roof. A small latrine is incorporated into the wall opposite the fire.

⓭ Gun Tower – Upper Gun Room

This room is in detail like the lower gun room. It is provided with reproduction guns and equipment to recreate the cramped, noisy and smoky conditions of the Tudor period. As there was a risk of explosion if the guns overheated through firing, or if a charge of gunpowder was placed in a hot gun, a supply of water was kept close by, fed from lead pipes that conducted rainwater off the roof.

By 1715 the room no longer contained guns: it had been partitioned into five bedrooms – one for the governor himself, the others possibly for his family or other officers. These were linked to his other apartments on the first floor of the forebuilding by a narrow passage cut through the tower wall.

⓮ Gun Tower – Roof Gun Platform

The open roof of the tower has seven embrasures and was also a gun platform. The lookout turret with its seven small windows was important for spotting ships at sea. It was covered by a lead cupola and provided with a fireplace for warmth. A short flight of steps leads to the forebuilding roof.

Left: Roof of Pendennis Castle showing the time ball that was dropped at 1pm every day as a signal to ships to set their clocks to GMT. From 1893 to 1909 the naval signal station on the roof relayed signals and orders to Royal Navy ships

Below left: Two of the gun ports in the upper gun room, with reproduction Tudor guns and equipment

Below: The arms of the Board of Ordnance on a 19th-century iron fireplace surround in the forebuilding. The Board was responsible for forts and all military supplies to the Army and Navy

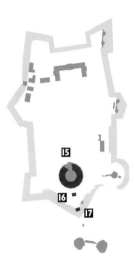

Below: The war shelter for One-Gun Battery, set out for a meal, with hammocks stowed away

15 Chemise

Reached from the forebuilding lobby, this is a broad platform built against the tower and faced in stone. It has embrasures for 14 guns, with recesses for shot between them. Two reproduction Tudor guns on wooden truck carriages are on display. The chemise replaced the lower gun room, providing greater firepower and more spacious and healthier working conditions for the gunners.

16 War Shelter

Covered by a large earth mound for protection against shellfire, this building was originally a gunpowder magazine built in about 1733. In about 1895 it was converted into a shelter for One-Gun Battery. Shelters were living areas for gunners on duty, day or night, where they ate and slept ready to 'stand to' their guns at a moment's notice. It is fitted-out to the period of the early 20th century as a simple practical space warmed by a small stove.

17 BATTERY OBSERVATION POST

The Battery Observation Post (BOP) was built in the Second World War to control the 6-inch guns of Half-Moon Battery below and has been restored to resemble its wartime appearance. It is a low concrete building sunk into the rampart for protection, with a glazed front and sides allowing a wide view of the sea.

Providing an accurate position for targets was vital. Before the 1880s this was achieved with difficulty using simple instruments and experience. In the 1880s optical instruments came into service that enabled accurate determination of the range and bearing of a moving target. The large instrument in the BOP is a reproduction depression position finder. Observations through the telescope could be plotted on a gridded map on the semicircular table underneath. By repeating readings it was possible to determine the course and speed of a ship and thereby to predict its future position. With corrections for wind and tide, the guns could be laid onto that position, so shells could be fired to land in the path of the moving enemy ship.

In the course of the Second World War information on the range and bearing of targets was set on dials and sent to the guns electrically by a system of motors and cables called Magslip transmission, appearing on numerical dials next to the guns. Some of the Magslip electrical equipment survives in the BOP.

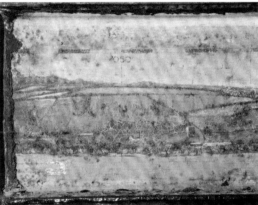

Top: The Battery Observation Post (BOP) for Half-Moon Battery, with communication equipment and charts, arranged as it may have been during the Second World War

Left: Captain Cliffe, the observation post officer in charge of Half-Moon Battery, inside the BOP during the Second World War

Above: Detail of a painting of the coastline above the observation post window, showing the area commanded by the guns

Right: Among a large collection of 19th- and 20th-century guns in Horse Pool Bastion is the monster 'Long Tom', seen here in blank firing

1 The 155mm 'Long Tom', a huge field gun used by US forces from 1943

2 Gun limber for 25-pounder field gun

3 British 25-pounder field gun, in use during and after the Second World War

4 Barr & Stroud optical range and height finder used with anti-aircraft guns in the First and Second World Wars

5 British 3-inch anti-aircraft gun in use from 1914 until the Second World War

Right: Half-Moon Battery today, with one of the 6-inch guns inside its camouflaged gunhouse

18 HALF-MOON BATTERY

The original battery, built in 1793, had the curved form of a half moon so that its guns covered a wide arc of fire to sea. It was repeatedly modified and from 1895 was rebuilt for two 6-inch BL 'disappearing' guns. These were removed in 1911, their gun pits filled and new 6-inch guns mounted to fire over a low parapet. The underground magazines and war shelter for the disappearing guns were retained and remain today, though their interiors were altered. They comprise most of the structure between the emplacements.

The guns were replaced twice during the Second World War, on the first occasion because the older guns were worn out, and on the second occasion by more modern types with greater range and power. The camouflaged concrete gun houses, which gave protection from aircraft, were added in 1941. Around the gun pits are lockers for supplies of ammunition brought up from the magazines, ready for action.

The guns on display are similar to those installed in 1943. They had a range of 12 miles and received target data from radar. At this time the battery had a staff of 99, of which 36 were on the guns, with the remainder on searchlights and position-finding cells or employed in communications.

19 HORSE POOL BASTION

This area contains a collection of guns from different periods, not all of which were used in the Falmouth defences. Three small guns on wooden platforms, looking out along the rampart, are carronades from the 19th century. They were used aboard ships and in fortresses for close defence, firing lethal showers of small metal balls.

The other guns on display are either field guns or anti-aircraft guns. There are two 25-pounder field guns, which were used by the British Army on campaign in the Second World War and afterwards. The largest gun is the 155mm 'Long Tom', a monster used by US forces as a heavy field gun from 1943 onwards.

A rarity is the first purpose-made British anti-aircraft gun, the 3-inch QF on its fixed steel pedestal. It entered service in 1914 and was still being used at the outbreak of the Second World War in 1939. It was largely replaced by the 3.7-inch gun, of which there is an example on display at East Bastion, on its 4-wheeled transport carriage. Finally there is the Swedish 40mm Bofors gun on its smaller mobile carriage, used by British forces as a light anti-aircraft gun during and after the Second World War.

The optical instrument standing on a tripod was used to find the height and range of aircraft. This information was then rapidly transmitted to the guns.

DEFENCES OUTSIDE THE FORT

A walk around the outside of the fort reveals the size of the Elizabethan ramparts and bastions, painstakingly revetted in local stone, though the ditch is now reduced in depth.

Further out on Pendennis Point are the remains of a small fort and gun positions, which originated in Tudor times. These were developed into a powerful sea battery until the late 18th century when Half-Moon Battery took over their role. Afterwards, the point remained in use for searchlights working with the guns at night.

20 Little Dennis Blockhouse

The most obvious survival on the point, and the oldest part of the defences, is Little Dennis – a squat Tudor blockhouse (gun tower) matched by another at St Mawes. It was built probably in 1539, just before Pendennis Castle itself. Its lower floor has three original gun embrasures in the curving seaward face, two of which were superseded by a fourth, larger embrasure in Tudor times. The rear wall has a fireplace and a large recess, perhaps a storage cupboard. In one corner are remains of a spiral stair to the upper floor and lookout turret.

The upper floor was open, with a deck made largely of timber. Only the rounded parapet survives, with embrasures for four more guns.

By 1600 the blockhouse was incorporated into the corner of a small walled and ditched fort enclosing all of Pendennis Point, which included three powerful gun batteries. In the 18th century, one of these was called Blockhouse Long Platform. It extended back along the shore towards Crab

Quay. Parts of its sea wall can be seen in eroding sections of the shoreline.

21 Crab Quay

Crab Quay was formed at the best landing point on the headland and was probably defended from Tudor times. By 1700 there was a guardhouse with a battery of guns that underwent many changes into the 20th century. Today it is possible to trace the outline of a rectangular banked and walled enclosure of the 19th-century battery. In its seaward face are two concrete emplacements for light 6-pounder QF guns built shortly after 1895, behind which are the stores of 1902 for shells and cartridges.

Left: Little Dennis Blockhouse, the earliest part of the defences on Pendennis Point, probably built in 1539
Below: *Crab Quay in the 1860s before its remodelling. Note the gun emplacements (centre), guardhouse (centre right) and limekiln in the foreground*

The Guns of Pendennis and St Mawes

Ships were armed with new, more powerful, rifled guns, capable of pulverizing coastal fortifications

Between the 1540s and 1940s the guns of Pendennis and St Mawes were changed several times to meet new threats. For most of this period the guns were cared for by a master gunner and worked by a small body of professional gunners from the government Artillery Train and, after 1716, the Royal Regiment of Artillery. These men were supplemented in wartime by local, part-time troops – the militia and the volunteers. Only in the 20th century were full, regular artillery units employed.

Smooth Bore Muzzle-Loading Guns
Before 1850 most gun barrels had smooth bores and were loaded at the front (muzzle). Fortress guns were often mounted on wheeled truck carriages and aimed using levers and wedges or elevating screws. Several such guns can be seen at Nine-Gun Battery at Pendennis and on the Saluting Battery at St Mawes. It required strength, skill and practice to work these

guns. Even in experienced hands they could be inaccurate and unreliable and so were grouped in batteries to increase the chance of hitting the target. From 1790 many coast guns were put on traversing slide carriages – wooden platforms on wheels that could be rotated around a fixed arc of iron rails and made aiming and firing easier and quicker.

The guns fired solid shot, canister and shell. Canisters of thin sheet metal contained small iron balls or stone fragments. The canisters disintegrated on firing, forming a lethal shower of iron and stone. Hollow shells, filled with gunpowder, exploded to scatter shards of fragmented casing.

In Tudor times high-quality bronze and cast-iron guns gradually replaced older and less reliable wrought-iron guns. The Alberghetti gun at St Mawes is a fine bronze piece made in about 1560. It would have been effective against warships, firing a 5-pound shot up to one mile. Pendennis has replicas of

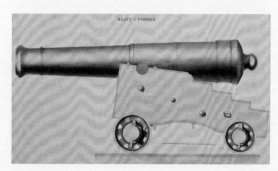

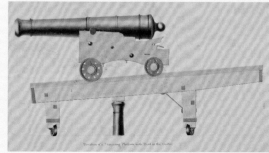

cast-iron guns of similar size and date, and both sites have replica wrought-iron swivel guns that were used for closer-range defence.

In 1715 these old guns (today called cannon), were still in use but were probably worn out. They were replaced soon after by new ones with more standard calibres. There are many 18th- and 19th-century examples at both sites, with calibres between 9- and 24-pounder. Pendennis has several carronades – a short gun introduced in 1779 used, in fortresses, for firing over short distances, scattering small shot against troops attacking the ramparts.

Rifled Breech-Loading Guns

In the 1850s the development of fast steam warships posed a great threat to coastal forts. These vessels could go almost anywhere, were not reliant on the wind, and had hulls protected with thick steel plate, against which conventional smooth-bore guns were ineffective. The ships were armed with new, more powerful, rifled guns, capable of pulverizing coastal fortifications. Consequently coastal forts were redesigned to withstand heavier bombardment, and were themselves equipped with these new guns.

The barrels of rifled guns were made with multiple spiral grooves (rifling) that caused pointed shells to spin, increasing stability and accuracy. More devastating shells were made of harder metal alloys, in an attempt to penetrate ships' side armour, and of more powerful explosives, to propel the shot over greater distances. At first rifled guns were mostly muzzle-loaders, but breech-loading (BL) systems soon followed and were perfected in the 1880s, becoming standard equipment in British coastal fortifications in the 1890s.

At this time BL rifled guns were installed nationwide, at the standard calibres of 6- and 10-inch, on 'disappearing' carriages as in One-Gun Battery at Pendennis. Within ten years these were replaced by 6- and 9.2-inch guns on fixed centre pivot mountings for easier operation. They fired up to 10 miles, like those in Half-Moon Battery. At the same time smaller guns were developed to deter fast light craft such as torpedo-carrying boats and small cruisers. These were called quick-firing (QF) guns, with calibres of 6- and 12-pounder; all appeared at Pendennis and St Mawes from the 1890s.

BL and QF guns were continually improved and remained in service in the Falmouth defences until the end of coast artillery in 1956.

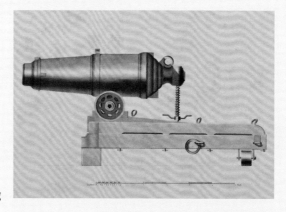

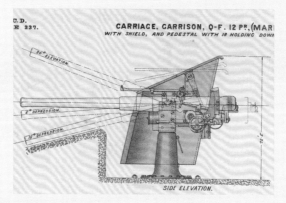

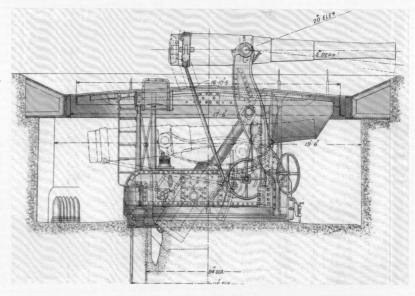

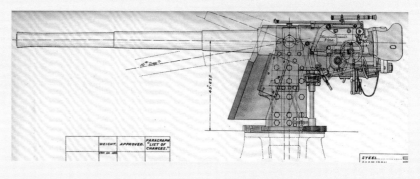

Left: The carronade was a devastating short cannon that fired lethal showers of small iron balls and fragments
Below left: A 12-pounder quick-firing gun of the type installed in the Falmouth defences from about 1890
Below: Victorian ingenuity introduced 'disappearing' guns that retracted after firing for reloading in the safety of a deep gun pit
Bottom: The modern gun: a 4.7-inch breech-loader from the 1890s. Although it proved too light for coastal defence (the 6-inch becoming standard), it had all the characteristics of the new design. On a fixed mounting it was quick and accurate

ST MAWES CASTLE SITE GUIDE

1 Guardhouse, bridge and entrance (page 20)

2,**5**–**8** Gun tower (pages 22–6)

3,**9** Forward bastion (pages 22–6)

4,**9** Side bastions (pages 22–6)

6 Roof and lookout turret (pages 23)

10 Exterior walls and ditch (page 26)

11 Grand Sea Battery and magazine (pages 26–8)

12 Tudor blockhouse (page 28)

13 Saluting battery (page 28)

Note: *Floor levels are not indicated on this illustration. See relevant numbers in the text for details.*

PARKING

- Visitor car park near entrance, with ramps for wheelchairs and prams

SITE ACCESS

- Level access to main entrance floor, shop and grounds. Battlements and bastions have no disabled access. Grass and tarmacked areas within the grounds

FACILITIES

- Shop with level access
- Picnics welcome; benches
- Accessible toilets

Tour of St Mawes Castle

Proud guardian of Carrick Roads, St Mawes Castle looks much as it did when built by Sir Thomas Treffry for Henry VIII in the 1540s, though it remained in use until 1956. In peacetime, a tiny garrison kept watch and maintained the guns, but in wartime it was full of soldiers. Its curving lines and compact form all but conceal its deadly purpose as a powerful platform for Henry's guns, a deterrent to hostile ships daring to brave the river passage. St Mawes is arguably the most perfect survivor of all Henry's forts: a careful design by a military engineer, executed by skilled masons and decorated with elegant carvings and verses that deliberately proclaim – and flatter – the Tudor monarchy. The castle comprises a tall, central, circular tower with three lower semicircular bastions attached to it in a trefoil plan. Outside, on the edge of the rocky shoreline, is a smaller semicircular Tudor blockhouse (gun tower). On the slope between it and the castle, the impressive Grand Sea Battery and magazine date largely from the Victorian era.

FOLLOWING THE TOUR

This tour divides into two parts: the first part covers the interior of the castle; the second includes the exterior and the gun batteries and blockhouse on the shoreline. The numbers beside the headings highlight the key points on the tour and correspond with the small numbered plans in the margins.

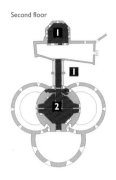

Second floor

Right: Carvings in the doorway spandrels on the second floor include Tudor roses, fleurs-de-lys and verse in praise of Henry VIII
Below: Detail of Henry VIII's family, in about 1545, by an unknown artist. Beside Henry is Prince Edward at the age of about seven (he became King Edward VI two years later) and Jane Seymour, Edward's mother, who had died several years earlier in 1537

◾ GUARDHOUSE, BRIDGE AND ENTRANCE

The approach to the castle is through the original guardhouse. It was an octagonal structure leading directly onto the bridge, altered to its present shape before 1735 by the addition of the elongated yard behind it.

The guardhouse could be defended with handguns through elaborate cross-shaped loops, and it had a fireplace for basic comfort. Beyond it, a twin-arched stone bridge crosses a rock-cut

ditch that originally extended around the castle to form an extra obstacle to an attack. Pillars rise from the bridge abutments onto its parapet and may have supported heraldic beasts or other symbols. The bridge leads to the arched entrance of the castle, which is flanked by cross-shaped handgun loops. There are also murder holes in the underside of the arch, through which defenders could fire at attackers at the gates.

Above the entrance are slots for drawbridge chains and a window that doubled as a gun position overlooking the bridge. Over the window is a fine carving of the Tudor royal arms and the first of several Latin inscriptions. This inscription adorns a stone cordon, with its carved gargoyles at regular intervals, which extends around the tower.

The inscription reads:
Semper honos Henrice tuus laudesque manebunt (Henry, thy honour and praises will remain forever)

The verses were composed in honour of Henry VIII and his son, Edward, by John Leland, a royal chaplain who was appointed 'King's Antiquary' to document the antiquities of all England. Leland spent the years 1540 to 1546 travelling and researching. His great work, published after his death as *The Itinerary*, was the first systematic description of the nation's historic buildings, monuments and manuscripts.

GUN TOWER
◾ Second-floor Rooms

The entrance leads into the second floor of the central tower. Just inside, on either side of the entrance, are square holes for a large timber drawbar which barred the door. To the left, a spiral stair connects all levels of the tower. To the right another stair leads onto the north side bastion, over a glass panel in the floor that covers a small chamber (an oubliette), where a prisoner may have been confined or an unruly soldier punished.

This floor was probably intended for the most important officers; in Tudor times the captain and his aides, and by 1828 a master gunner and his assistants, who maintained the guns. It is divided by partition on original lines into three comfortable rooms: two smaller rooms are located on either side of a corridor that leads to a third, larger room.

Smuggling and Piracy on the Cornish Coast

Until modern times Cornwall was a remote and poor rural county and buying goods without paying duty to the Crown (smuggling) and seizing ships (piracy) were part of everyday life for whole communities – gentlemen and labourers alike. In 1753 George Borlase of Penzance commented 'The coasts here swarm with smugglers from the Land's End to the Lizard'.

The government of Elizabeth I (1558–1603) quietly encouraged piracy on Spanish ships both as a means of unofficial warfare and as a ready source of revenue. Far from being an activity of desperate renegades, it was controlled by the rich and well-connected. Although a commission was appointed to investigate piracy in Cornwall, it was a sham, being chaired by Sir John Killigrew (c.1554–1605), who was a pirate himself. In the winter of 1580–81 a merchant ship, forced into Falmouth by a storm, was plundered by pirates. Sir John was suspected, summoned before the Privy Council and ordered to return the stolen goods. In later, perhaps embroidered accounts, his wife Lady Killigrew was rumoured to have boarded the ship herself, with 'a numerous party of ruffians', who murdered the Spanish merchants on board for two barrels of Spanish pieces of eight (silver coin).

The English were not alone; most European maritime nations were involved and the Cornish were often on the receiving end. The notorious Barbary pirates from North Africa raided the English coast for plunder and slaves: between

'The coasts here swarm with smugglers from the Land's End to the Lizard'
George Borlase, 1753

1616 and 1642 they took some 350 to 400 English ships and between 6,500 and 7,000 prisoners, half of them from the West Country. One Thomas Pellow from Penryn was captured at the age of 10 in 1715 and was a slave for 23 years in Rabat, Morocco, before making his escape.

Falmouth smugglers operated brazenly in the 18th century. In 1762 three ships of the East India Company held a fortnight-long bazaar, selling all manner of oriental luxury goods, duty-free. The Falmouth packet ships operated a mail-order service for contraband goods.

Piracy in English waters was brought to an end in the 19th century by determined campaigns of patrol and capture by Customs Officers and the Royal Navy.

Above: A 17th-century engraving of the Barbarossa brothers, Aruj and Khizir, Barbary pirates who gained notoriety for their ferocious activities in the 16th century
Below: French Smugglers Detected by Custom House Officers at Landing, by Thomas Rowlandson, 1790

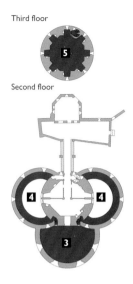

Third floor

Second floor

Above: The Alberghetti gun (foreground) and a 19th-century gun, on gun platforms on the ground floor of the forward bastion
Below: Detail of the barrel of the Alberghetti gun, showing the initials of the maker, S. A. (Sigismondo Alberghetti)

All three have carved panels over the door heads: the one leading to the large room features two heads and the English inscriptions 'God save King Henry VIII' and 'God save Prince Edward' – an expression of loyalty to all visitors.

All the rooms have windows and fireplaces. The fireplace in the main room has an alcove above it, possibly for a coat of arms, and smaller openings on either side were for storage.

🄷 Forward Bastion – Gun Platform

A wide doorway at the far end of the large room, also with drawbar holes and murder holes, leads onto the open roof of the forward bastion. This has a parapet with four embrasures for guns which could command the river. The round sockets in the sills of the embrasures indicate small breech-loading handguns on swivel mountings, while recesses between embrasures were for small amounts of shot and powder kept for quick use. Over the door outside Henry VIII's royal arms are carved in stone with sculptures on each side – possibly mermen – above an inscription in Latin that reads:

> *Semper vivet anima Regis Henrici Octavi qui anno 34 sui regni hoc fecit fieri* (May the soul of King Henry VIII, who had this built in the 34th year of his reign, live forever).

🄸 Side Bastions – Upper Levels

From the roof of the forward bastion, short flights of steps lead up through the doorways onto wall-walks on both side bastions. Off the steps to the south bastion is a small latrine for the gunners on duty: slots in the stonework indicate the position of a wooden seat. Both side bastions are hollow to ground level and reveal the full height of the central tower. Their parapets each have five embrasures for swivel guns and the usual ammunition recesses.

🄵 Third Floor

This comprises one large room and may have been where the garrison slept. It was also defensible by small breech-loading guns, like the one displayed, by hackbutts (early muskets), and by bows and arrows. The walls contain eight arched positions for guns, with smoke vents in their vaults and the familiar ammunition recesses in the side walls. The embrasures are formed into windows with decorative pointed arches.

In 1828 it was estimated that the room could sleep 70 men in hammocks. As late as 1905 it was designated for 20 men who in wartime would operate the quick-fire guns on the sea battery; it contained two coal-fired cooking ranges, a fly-proof larder, and mop and plate racks.

6 Roof and Lookout Turret

The roof was designed as a platform for seven guns firing through embrasures in the parapet, which also incorporates the smoke vent outlets from the floor below. A small turret formed a lookout position and has four small windows, originally with internal shutters.

7 Basement – Kitchen and Storeroom

This level of the tower was originally partitioned into a kitchen and storerooms, and remained so for most of its history, though in emergencies it would have accommodated up to 20 men. At the base of the steps is an octagonal granite table, perhaps used to hold food and drink before it was taken up to mess. A wall recess next to it may have held a cistern filled from a well immediately outside. This collected water seeping from the rock face. The large kitchen fireplace has a bread oven built into one corner and an adjacent recess in the wall probably held utensils. Of six windows, two extend to floor level and may have incorporated storage facilities.

8 First Floor – Mess and Living Space

Also originally partitioned, this floor was intended as the daily living space and mess for the garrison. But for most of its life until the second half of the 19th century, it was used as a gunpowder storeroom – a precarious situation for the garrison. In wartime it could accommodate 20 men.

The room is brightly lit by large windows and has two fireplaces and a small cubicle, perhaps a latrine.

9 Forward and Side Bastions – Lower Floor

A large doorway leads to steps from the first floor to the ground floor of the forward bastion. Most of the heavy guns were emplaced in the forward bastion, in vaulted positions with smoke vents and

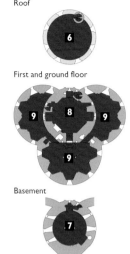

Left and below right: Details from an 18th-century copy of the lost 16th-century murals from Cowdray House, showing gunners on the roof of Southsea Castle, one of Henry VIII's coastal forts (left) and soldiers of Henry VIII's army carrying hackbutts (matchlock muskets) (below right)

Below left: The basement kitchen at St Mawes, showing the fireplace with a bread oven built into the corner

FLOOR PLANS OF ST MAWES CASTLE

Third-floor Gun Tower

Gun room

Second-floor Gun Tower and
Bastions Parapet Level

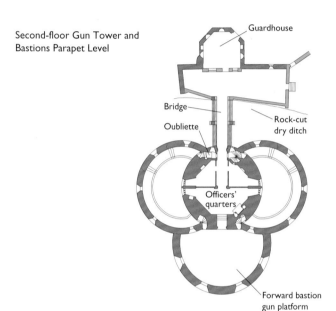

Guardhouse

Bridge

Oubliette

Rock-cut
dry ditch

Officers'
quarters

Forward bastion
gun platform

First-floor Gun Tower and
Ground-floor Bastions

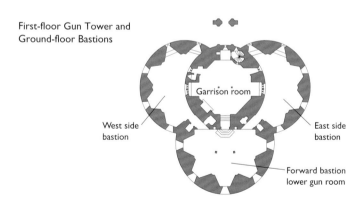

Garrison room

West side
bastion

East side
bastion

Forward bastion
lower gun room

Gun Tower Basement

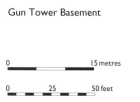

Kitchen and
storeroom

0   15 metres

0   25   50 feet

■ 1539–45

■ 18th century
and later

KEY

1 Guardhouse
2 Bridge
3 Rock-cut dry ditch
4 Lookout turret
5 Roof gun platform
6 Third-floor gun room
7 Second-floor officers' quarters
8 First-floor garrison room
9 Basement kitchen and storeroom
10 Forward bastion gun platform
11 Forward bastion lower gun room
12 East side bastion
13 West side bastion

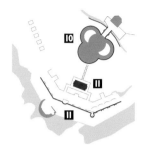

Above: One of three carved shields on the outside of the castle. Above them, from east round to west, inscriptions read:

Gaudeat Edwardo nunc duce Cornubia felix *(Rejoice happy Cornwall now that Edward is duke)*

Honora Henricum Octavum Angli Francie et Hibernie regum excellentissum *(Honour Henry VIII, most excellent king of England, France and Ireland)*

Edwardus fama referat factisque parentum *(May Edward resemble his father in fame and deeds)*

Right: The Grand Sea Battery, of 1880, with a gun on a replica traversing platform

Facing page: St Mawes Castle, showing the full extent of the Grand Sea Battery and the shoreline blockhouse (centre and centre left)

square embrasures. From here, they commanded the river across to Pendennis. Many of the guns on display are 18th-century but the cast bronze piece, recovered from the sea near Teignmouth in Devon, is a 'saker' (a saker is a bird of prey – many early guns were named after birds). It was made in about 1560 by a Venetian gunsmith called Alberghetti. Similar guns were used at St Mawes and fired shot of about 5lb (2.26kg) in weight up to a mile.

Small passages connect the forward bastion to the side bastions. Off each passage are two small rooms. These were all latrines except one in the north passage, which may have been a magazine. The side bastions each have four gun positions, two for heavy guns and two with cross-shaped loops for handguns.

10 EXTERIOR WALLS

Outside, the rock-cut ditch and bridge can be properly viewed, and a drip-well for water seeping through the rocks lies under the landward side of the bridge. Each external face of the bastion is adorned with a large crowned shield in carved stonework. These were probably brightly painted and decorated and are large enough to be seen from the river passage. With their inscriptions, set out in the caption to the left, they are a clear proclamation of Edward as Henry's heir to the throne and as overlord of Cornwall.

11 GRAND SEA BATTERY AND MAGAZINE

In Tudor times the castle guns were supported by more guns at the shoreline, firing from the blockhouse and from open platforms behind a parapet. By the early 18th century the castle was essentially a barracks and gunpowder store, and most of the guns were emplaced in what became known in the 19th century as the Grand Sea Battery. This battery was rebuilt several times to meet new threats, with the surviving arrangements dating from between 1850 and 1905.

Concern about the risk of a garrison living side-by-side with gunpowder in the castle resulted in a new main magazine (ammunition store). This was built in 1854, in a rock-cut terrace recessed into the hillside for protection, and reached down steep steps from the castle. The thick walls and the floor of the magazine are pierced by ventilation slots to prevent excessive moisture, which would spoil the powder. Inside, it was lined with wood and divided into two rooms with separate entrances in the gables. One room contained gunpowder made up into fabric bags (cartridges); the other held the explosive shells. Smaller supplies of both were kept in expense (ready-use) magazines closer to the guns in case of a surprise attack.

At the same time the sea battery was rebuilt as a broad, open and sunken gun floor, its sides lined

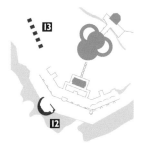

Right: The Tudor blockhouse at St Mawes, viewed from the sea and showing one of the gun embrasures of the lower floor

Below: Late 18th-century and early 19th-century guns on reproduction truck carriages, forming a saluting battery

in stone. The front has three faces for 12 shell-firing guns that were mounted on wheeled wooden platforms, known as traversing platforms. These pivoted at the front to enable a wide arc of fire through the granite embrasures. The rear wall has three alcoves that were used for mobile furnaces, in which solid shot was brought to a red heat for firing at the decks and rigging of ships. A burning ship was among the greatest of sailors' fears.

By 1880 the battery was remodelled for four 64-pounder rifled muzzle-loading guns (RMLs), also on traversing platforms, whose racers can still be seen in a group on the eastern face of the battery. Their embrasures remain open. The gun on display, a 12-pounder of about 1815, is set up on the original racers to resemble the 64-pounder arrangement. The traversing platform and slide carriage allowed the gun to recoil smoothly for reloading. Eight of the old embrasures for the shell

guns of the 1850s were blocked at this time, but many of the iron gun pivots remain.

A final chapter in the gun story is provided by two more emplacements let into the sea battery. The first is circular and recessed into the parapet at the junction of the eastern and central faces. It was for a light quick-firing (QF) breech-loading (BL) gun of 1891, designed to protect the river against fast torpedo boats and lightly armoured destroyers. It may have been modified for a machine gun. The second is a platform built against the central face, the sole survivor of a pair of later 6-pounder QF guns that were used between 1898 and 1903, when they were withdrawn because they were not powerful enough for their role.

12 TUDOR BLOCKHOUSE

This is the twin of the blockhouse at Pendennis Point, together perhaps forming the first defence for Carrick Roads in the late 1530s. It is built into a rock-cut platform on the shoreline, as a D-shaped gun tower of two floors. The upper floor, which was a wooden deck open to the sky, does not survive. The ground floor has four gun ports (one blocked), a fireplace, an oven and a water cistern.

13 SALUTING BATTERY

In the western part of the site, five guns of late 18th- and 19th-century date are on display on reproduction wooden platforms as a saluting battery. Historically, these batteries fired salutes on important ceremonial occasions, as part of national celebrations and to honour important visitors.

St Anthony Head

For centuries there have been buildings on St Anthony Head to assist ships in navigation. They culminated in the still-functioning St Anthony lighthouse, built by Trinity House in 1835.

St Anthony Battery

In 1796 St Anthony Battery was built on the rocky headland as part of a national programme to strengthen the most vulnerable coastal locations under threat of invasion from Napoleonic France. Its position at the extremity of the Fal estuary and clear of the main anchorage of Carrick Roads was ideal for providing extended protection against marauding warships. It comprised four powerful 32-pounder guns that remained in service until the end of war with France in 1815.

After the end of the Napoleonic wars there were periodic proposals for a permanent battery on St Anthony Head, but nothing happened until 1895, when a new battery was begun for two 6-inch guns, so extending the range of protection for Falmouth far out to sea. Because of its isolated location, the new battery on St Anthony Head became an extensive installation, with many support buildings for its garrison within a defended perimeter.

Twentieth-Century Service

By 1911 the Admiralty had moved their Port War Signal Station from Pendennis to a new building at St Anthony Head. It was one of many such naval lookout and communications centres established at major ports in time of war. They played a vital part in defence by locating enemy ships, relaying naval orders and helping to co-ordinate naval and military forces in action. The men were skilled signallers using flags, flashing lamps and wireless telegraph.

The battery at St Anthony was periodically updated and was operational in the 20th century during both world wars, in conjunction with St Mawes and Pendennis, as part of an integrated defence plan for the whole estuary. In 1943 a second group of three 6-inch guns was completed nearby and called Roseland Battery. The site was decommissioned by the army in 1956 and is now cared for by the National Trust. Remains of the gun emplacements and support buildings can still be seen.

Left: Troops aboard SS Guinean approaching Falmouth, June 1940, probably evacuated from France during Operation Aerial. The lighthouse at St Anthony Head can be seen in the background

Below: Painting by John Platt, 1942, of a convoy passing St Anthony Head. During the battle of the Atlantic, Falmouth Harbour was often the first port of call for merchant ships and their escorts after the dangerous journey across the ocean

History

Pendennis and St Mawes witnessed
remarkable events in their 400-year service.
Established during Henry VIII's fortress building
of the 1540s, they kept watch as the massed
ships of the Armada sailed by on their way
to destruction in 1588. Pendennis narrowly
escaped Spanish revenge when another
powerful fleet was turned back by bad
weather on its way to take the castle in 1596.

In 1646 the Civil War brought severe
military action to Pendennis. Prince Charles
(later King Charles II) used the castle as
refuge, on his way abroad to escape his
opposition. Shortly afterwards Pendennis

saw remnants of the royalist forces surrender
to the parliamentary army.

After the restoration of the monarchy
in 1660 Falmouth developed as a port, mail
packet station and harbour. Its strategic
position ensured that its defences were
maintained and updated, forming an
increasingly powerful operational base. It
saw service during the Napoleonic and both
World Wars, when it was a convoy port for
the Atlantic crossing and a base for offensive
action. The most daring operation was
the raid mounted from Falmouth on the
German docks at St Nazaire in 1942.

DEFENDING THE GREAT ANCHORAGE (1540–1956)

The headland of Pendennis and the point at St Mawes greet each other across the mouth of the river Fal, a wide, deep estuary known as Carrick Roads. With the exploration of the 'New World' in the late 15th and 16th centuries, the estuary emerged as the first and last safe haven for shipping crossing the Atlantic or coming north from the Mediterranean. It remained an important strategic port for some 450 years. That period witnessed an almost continuous and complex struggle for power among many nations – particularly England, France, Spain, Holland, Germany and, later, America. England was allied with or fighting against all these nations at different times, resulting in piracy, raiding and warfare around the coast, in far-flung colonies, in continental Europe and around the world. This explains the continuous development of fortifications at Pendennis and St Mawes between 1540 and 1956: it was vital to defend the estuary from foreign nations to prevent its use as a supply base for attack or invasion.

THE HENRICIAN ARTILLERY FORTS

By the 1530s, relations between England, France and Spain had deteriorated due to Henry VIII's (1509–47) divorce from his first wife, Catherine of Aragon, and the ensuing religious rift with Rome and the Catholic Church. At this time, piracy and naval warfare were commonplace, tolerated and even encouraged by seafaring nations. One such incident occurred in 1537 when Spanish and French ships fought each other along Carrick Roads as far as Truro. Afterwards, an important local gentleman, John Arundell of Trerice, petitioned the king for guns in 'blockhouses made upon our haven, else we shall have more of the same'.

Two years passed without action, until England became isolated politically following the formal alliance of France and Spain in 1538. The prospect of invasion prompted action on a national scale. Henry VIII sent commissioners across the country to assess the most vulnerable parts of the coastline. This resulted in a grand and expensive plan, the 'Device of the King', to build 30 new

Above: Francis I, king of France (1515–47), and Henry VIII's great rival, by Joos van Cleve
Left: Henry VIII in 1540, aged 49, by Hans Holbein the Younger
Below: Detail from an 18th-century copy of the lost 16th-century Cowdray murals, showing Southsea Castle in Portsmouth at the time of the sinking of the Mary Rose, in 1545. The castle was built during the last part of Henry's defence plan, the 'Device of the King'

Facing page: A chart of Falmouth Haven made in the 16th century, probably for defensive purposes

Above: Detail of a map of the south-west coast of England made between 1539 and 1540 to indicate where enemy landings could be made. Annotations made on the map in 1541 describe St Mawes as 'half made', and Pendennis headland is fortified only by a ditch

Right: A design of 1539 for one of Henry VIII's 'Device' forts. Its central tower and surrounding tiers of symmetrical bastions are characteristic of all Henry VIII's south-coast forts

fortifications to protect vulnerable ports, anchorages and landing places on the south and east coasts. Carrick Roads was important to England as a base for mounting naval and privateering operations, and to her enemies as a potential bridgehead from which to mount an invasion. This is why Pendennis and St Mawes castles were on Henry's list.

On the south side of Carrick Roads, Pendennis was an ideal defensive location, connected to the mainland by a narrow neck of land. The earliest map of the area, of about 1540, depicts a ditch across this little isthmus, isolating the headland. Although this may have been a defensive earthwork of Tudor times, the ancient name of the site, Pen Dinas or 'the fort on the headland', suggests that it may have had an earlier origin, perhaps part of a prehistoric or early historic fort.

By 1540 gunpowder artillery was established as a powerful weapon of war. Guns on either side of the entrance provided the most effective defence for Carrick Roads, threatening ships by crossfire. Two small gun towers, or blockhouses, close to the shoreline at St Mawes and Pendennis, were probably built just before the main castles. They may, however, also have been just one part

of the wider defensive plan, sited to fire on shipping at close range.

The main castles were artillery forts built in the period between 1540 and 1545. They were elegantly planned for 360 degree defence by guns mounted at several levels. The design of all 30 forts was a work of government controlled by Henry himself, influenced by specialist military engineers, one of whom was a German, Stephan von Hapschenburg. Although the forts were planned for all-round fire, their primary purpose was offensive, with guns to fire on warships. In some cases, however, the circular designs created blind spots in the field of fire against enemies attacking close-by, on land, making the forts in these situations an easy target for enemy guns.

St Mawes was particularly vulnerable to a land attack from high ground to the east, though it is possible, as at Pendennis, that earthwork defences were made to counter such approaches. Though without doubt powerful forts, they were a blind alley in military design, and within ten years were eclipsed by low-lying forts, employing angular bastions, which had emerged in Italy by 1500. This system more effectively balanced the offensive and defensive elements of fortress design.

Cornwall in Tudor Times

Building the forts presented some difficulties. In Tudor times Cornwall was a long way from the centre of government in London. Its people spoke

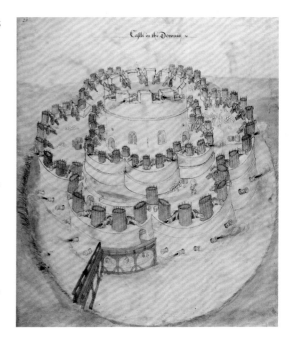

The Killigrews of Arwenack

The Killigrews were an ancient Cornish family who were living at the manor of Arwenack, in the lee of Pendennis, shortly before 1400. They were prominent in local Cornish matters, and occasionally at national level in the business of state, until the male line died out in the late 17th century.

Henry VIII built Pendennis Castle on Arwenack land, making John Killigrew (d.1567) its first captain in the 1540s. One of his five sons, Sir John Killigrew (d.1584), succeeded him in the post, as did his own son, also John (c.1554–1605). As captains, the Killigrews were responsible for the garrison, for raising local forces during emergencies and for the defence of the estuary, most notably against Spain in the 1580s and 1590s.

Despite this role of public responsibility, the Killgrews, in common with many gentlemen seafarers of the day, financed and took part in piracy. They did so from a base near Pendennis, on the Helford river, and profited greatly, but the blatant activities of the third John (d.1605) eventually became an embarrassment to the government. He was lured to London in 1597 on the pretext of discussing new fortifications at Pendennis and although promptly arrested he escaped serious punishment, perhaps due to family influence at court.

Notable for more distinguished service to the Crown are the brother of Sir John, Sir Henry Killigrew (c.1525–1603), and John's great-nephew Sir William Killigrew (d.1695). Sir Henry served as a diplomatic agent of Elizabeth I in France, Germany and Scotland and Sir William commanded one of the king's cavalry regiments in the Civil War, leading a famous charge at the battle of Edgehill in 1642.

The Killigrews rebuilt their home, Arwenack, in 1567, and included defensive features, such as rectangular ports for small guns. It was badly damaged by fire in the early stages of the siege of Pendennis Castle in 1646. Rebuilt after the war and extended after 1786, it survives today.

> The Killigrews, in common with many gentlemen seafarers of the day, financed and took part in piracy

Right: Philip II, king of Spain (1556–98), in about 1557, by Sir Anthonis Mor van Dashorst (Antonio Moro). Philip entered into a war against England that culminated in the Spanish Armada of 1588

Below: Map of Falmouth Haven of 1579. The castles are carefully drawn. Note the lead cupola that then covered the lookout turret of Pendennis and the short-lived, twin-towered forebuilding

their own language and possessed their own distinctive identity, which was more Cornish than English. As a Venetian ambassador remarked of Carrick Roads in 1506: 'We are in a very wild place which no human being ever visits … in the midst of a most barbarous race, so different in language and customs from the Londoners and the rest of England that they are as intelligible to these last as to the Venetians.' Nevertheless, Cornwall had a thriving economy based on tin mining and fishing, and a prosperous gentry who exercised great influence over local affairs.

The Building of Pendennis and St Mawes

At this time of prosperity the building was entrusted to eminent local gentlemen under the guidance of government officers and design drawings. In 1540 Lord Admiral Russell, the king's officer in the south-west, appointed Sir Thomas Treffry of Fowey to build St Mawes Castle. The builder of Pendennis is unknown but its different construction suggests another hand. The prime candidate is John Killigrew of Arwenack, on whose land it was built.

Left: English ships fighting the Spanish Armada of 1588, possibly off Gravelines, the only large-scale battle of the conflict (English school, 16th century)

Below: Detail of Queen Elizabeth I (1558–1603) in about 1575–80, when the threat of invasion by Spain was great, by an unknown artist of the English school

St Mawes remains largely as built, a three-storey tower with three semicircular bastions arranged symmetrically. Pendennis was originally intended to be a freestanding circular gun tower of three storeys, but was modified during construction to incorporate the chemise. This was a low circular earth platform around the base of the tower to mount guns in the open behind a parapet. It replaced the guns of the ground floor, which no longer had a clear field of fire. When complete, both forts were properly supplied and fully garrisoned only when there was a threat of conflict.

THE ELIZABETHAN FORTRESSES

In 1569, political and religious differences between England and Spain, aggravated by piracy and raiding on the high seas and in the Americas, led to war. Pendennis and St Mawes were garrisoned, provisioned and provided with guns. The gathering of a Spanish invasion fleet at Santander in 1574 prompted further emergency measures, including earthworks to protect the landward approaches to Pendennis; by 1579 there was a bank and ditch crossing the headland 400m north-west of the fort, with an entrance flanked by two small,

semicircular bastions. At the same time, the blockhouse on Pendennis Point had an additional battery of guns extending the field of fire upriver; which may also have been the case at St Mawes. In 1578 each fort was garrisoned by 100 men.

The Spanish invasion plans of 1579 faltered when England's great ally, bad weather, intervened. Nine years later, the Great Armada of 1588 sailed by and up the English Channel to meet destruction by English ships and stormy weather. Hostilities continued and with many Cornish gentlemen involved in piracy, punitive coastal raids by Spanish forces based in Brittany resulted in the burning of the Killigrew's house at Arwenack in 1593, and the partial burning of Penzance, Newlyn, Paul and Mousehole in 1595. In 1596 another huge fleet assembled in Spain under the command of Martin de Padilla, the Governor (Adelantado) of Castile, bent on taking Pendennis, fortifying the headland and using Carrick Roads as a springboard for a prolonged campaign on English soil. This new armada was turned away again, by bad weather, but the threat forced the government of Queen Elizabeth I (1558–1603) to review the defences; Sir Walter Raleigh's

The Growth of Falmouth

When Pendennis Castle was built in the 1540s Falmouth did not exist. There was only the Killigrew manor house of Arwenack, a few cottages called Smithwick and an ale house named Peny-cwm-cuic. John Killigrew began to extend Smithwick in 1613, but was stopped temporarily by a petition to the king from the towns of Penryn, Truro, and Helston, which feared loss of their trade from a new settlement on the river. King James I, however, allowed Killigrew to continue and building quickly resumed. In 1653 a weekly market was established and in 1661 Smithwick, renamed Falmouth, received a town charter from Charles II. By 1664 there were 200 houses in the town.

In 1688 Falmouth became a Royal Mail packet station from which fast sailing ships carried mail to Spain and the Mediterranean, and later to the West Indies and North and South America. Carrying and protecting mail was an expensive, though lucrative, business and, with trade flourishing in goods of all kinds, Falmouth became the largest port in Cornwall. Perhaps the most famous message received at the port was the first news of the great naval victory at Trafalgar and the death of Vice-Admiral Lord Nelson, which reached Falmouth on 4 November 1805 in the hands of Lieutenant Lapenotière of HMS *Pickle*, who continued with it at speed overland to London.

On a visit to Falmouth in June 1809, just four years after Nelson's victory at Trafalgar, the poet Lord Byron (1788–1824) wrote to his friend Francis Hodgson:

This town of Falmouth, as you will partly conjecture, is no great ways from the sea. It is defended on the sea-side by tway castles, St. Maws and Pendennis, extremely well calculated for annoying every body except an enemy. St. Maws is garrisoned by an able-bodied person of fourscore, a widower. He has the whole command and sole management of six most unmanageable pieces of ordnance, admirably adapted for the destruction of Pendennis, a like tower of strength on the opposite side of the Channel. We have seen St. Maws, but Pendennis they will not let us behold, save at a distance, because Hobhouse and I are suspected of having already taken St. Maws by a coup de main.

The town contains many Quakers and salt fish – the oysters have a taste of copper, owing to the soil of a mining country – the women (blessed be the Corporation therefor!) are flogged at the cart's tail when they pick and steal, as happened to one of the fair sex yesterday noon. She was pertinacious in her behaviour, and damned the mayor.

Falmouth's mail ships traversed the globe until 1852, when the service was transferred to Southampton. Though loss of the mail was keenly felt, from 1861 Falmouth Docks were developed and trade was helped by railway connections established in 1863.

The docks and railway brought new prosperity from both trade and tourists, who came to enjoy the beaches. In 1865 the first major hotel, the Falmouth Hotel, was built west of Pendennis headland. Beatrix Potter, who was to become famous for her children's books, stayed at the hotel in 1894. While there she saw a pig on board a ship in the harbour and wrote to a young friend, illustrating the pig's imagined escape from the ship's cook and subsequent adventures, in the style that was later to become her trademark. The pig contributed to her inspiration for her book *The Tale of Little Pig Robinson*, which, although only published in 1930, was one of the first she wrote.

Tourism remains a feature of the town, which is still flourishing, its harbour a busy scene of ship repair, visiting ocean liners and much other commercial and leisure traffic.

'It is defended on the sea-side by tway castles, St. Maws and Pendennis, extremely well calculated for annoying every body except an enemy'
Lord Byron, 1809

Above: Lord Byron in 1814, *by Thomas Phillips*
Left: Strachan's Action after Trafalgar, *showing four prize ships of the defeated Franco–Spanish fleet being taken to Falmouth in November 1805. Pendennis Castle can be seen in the background*

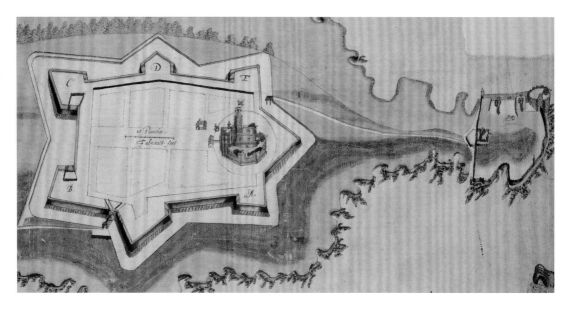

Right: The earliest known plan of Paul Ive's bastioned fort and sea 'bulwark' on Pendennis headland. Although not showing the fort exactly as built, it is close enough, and thought to be contemporary with building in 1597–1600

Below: Sir Walter Raleigh, 1598, by William Segar. Raleigh, Sir Nicholas Parker and Sir Ferdinando Gorges surveyed Pendennis in 1597 and commissioned a new fortress from Ive against the threat of Spanish invasion

muster of 500 men at Pendennis would have been no match for a Spanish force said to be of about 20,000.

Shortly after the failed Spanish attack, in 1597 the experienced soldier Sir Nicholas Parker surveyed Pendennis with Raleigh and Sir Ferdinando Gorges, who had been building fortifications in Plymouth. They proposed a new fortress to command the whole headland and gave its design to Paul Ive, an exceptional engineer who had built fortifications in the Low Countries in the 1570s and in the Channel Islands in the 1590s, employing the

Italian angle bastion system. He supervised the costly building of a new fortress at Pendennis between 1597 and 1600 using 400 local men. It is depicted on a plan of about 1611 as an elongated pentagon with a rampart and ditch, with a full or half-bastion at each angle and a large triangular southern end overlooking Pendennis Point, where the old blockhouse was incorporated into another small fort. The main Henrician castle was retained at the south-eastern end of the new fortress.

St Mawes may also have been given two angle bastions, described in 1623 as 'two angled Bullwerks' of earth and timber with gun platforms, built out from the base of the Henrician fort.

Just as these new works were completed, there was peace with Spain and France for the first 20 years of the 17th century, following the union of England and Scotland under King James I (1603–25). Garrisons nationwide were reduced or neglected and guns were removed to London or dismounted. The garrison at St Mawes was only 14 strong and that of Pendennis impoverished through lack of pay; they reportedly resorted to eating limpets and pawning bedding to pay for food. But in 1624, during a bitter series of conflicts in Europe called the Thirty Years War, England allied with France and Holland, declaring war against Spain. This prompted repairs at Pendennis and the construction of a new earthwork defence across the neck of the peninsula, by the engineer Sir Bernard Johnson in 1627. This was a rampart and ditch with powerful bastions and mounted guns to keep an enemy well away from the main fortress.

THE SIEGE OF PENDENNIS, 1646

The defences of Pendennis were not tested until the first Civil War between King Charles I (1625–49) and Parliament, which raged across Britain between 1642 and 1646. Falmouth became an important supply point for Charles's army. Vital imports of military equipment poured into the port from England and the Continent, paid for in part by Cornish tin. The guns of Pendennis and St Mawes watched over Carrick Roads and 15 warships used it as a base for preying on parliamentary shipping in the Channel.

The West Country was loyal to the king but as the tide of war turned in favour of Parliament, especially after the battle of Naseby in 1645, royalist forces in the south were gradually hunted down. Pendennis became one of the last royalist garrisons as the broken remnants of the royalist western army were forced deeper into the south-west. Pendennis was prepared as a winter quarters for Prince Charles (the future King Charles II (1660–85)) from October 1645, with new works to strengthen and extend the fortifications, notably a new outer strongpoint at Upton's Mount. Charles's mother, Queen Henrietta Maria, had stayed briefly at Pendennis before her escape to France in July 1644, and Prince Charles spent several weeks at Pendennis early in 1646.

At the beginning of March the royalist army was decisively defeated at Bovey Heath and at Torrington, both in Devon, and shortly afterwards, on 15 March, surrendered to the parliamentary commander, Lord Fairfax, at Tresillian Bridge, Truro.

Although Prince Charles left Pendennis on 2 March for safety on the Isles of Scilly, desperate plans were made to counter-attack from Pendennis with support from the Continent. About 1,000 troops gathered within the ramparts, but with no support coming, they dug in for the expected siege. As Fairfax approached, the tiny garrison of St Mawes surrendered, knowing it could not hold out against his large army. At Pendennis, recognizing the strength of the defences and the determination of the garrison, Fairfax's troops enclosed the peninsula with earthworks and gun batteries, and a regular bombardment was begun. The garrison responded with the fort guns and 40 more in a

Left: Prince Charles (later King Charles II), after Adriaen Hanneman, in about 1648, two years after his short stay at Pendennis

Below: *The parliamentary commander, Thomas Fairfax, by William Faithorne (after Robert Walke). In 1646 Fairfax's army forced the surrender of St Mawes and took Pendennis after a five-month siege*

Bottom: *Pendennis headland and the emerging town of Falmouth. This later print was based on an original made probably before 1645*

Right: A reconstruction by Ivan Lapper of Pendennis as it may have looked during the siege of 1646. Note the hornwork (a form of outer defence) and the 'traverses' — earthern ramparts running down from the castle to the sea to strengthen the land defences

Below: Colonel Christian Lilly's second survey of St Mawes Castle in 1735, showing St Mawes from the south-east

warship deliberately beached north of the fortress. After three months, food supplies in the fort began to run short and the commander, Sir John Arundell (b.1576), and his son Richard (1616–87), had to negotiate despite the opposition of some of his 800 men, with their 200 women and children. On 15 August terms were agreed and the garrison gave up its cannon and military stores but was allowed an honourable surrender, marching out two days later 'with flying colours, trumpets sounding, drums beating, matches lighted at both ends, bullets in the mouthes, and every souldier 12 charges of powder, with bullets and match proportionable, with all their own goods, bags and baggage, with a safe convoy into Arwinick Downs'.

THE LATE SEVENTEENTH CENTURY

After the dramatic siege, there were no major events at Pendennis and St Mawes in the remainder of the 17th century. There were plans to modernize the defences crossing the neck of the peninsula at Pendennis and the fort on Pendennis Point was reinforced with a new battery at Crab Quay. In the 1690s, however, there was a prolonged state of alert following the accession of William III as king of England (1689–1702). The French supported the political and Catholic religious policies of the deposed King James II (1685–88) and his 'Jacobite' supporters in England, Scotland and Ireland, seeing James as having absolute right to rule as the rightful heir of the Stuart line. The French endeavoured to replace William and war followed. Although French forces landed once at Teignmouth in Devon, it came to nothing and in 1697 France reluctantly accepted William as king.

Against this background, the maintenance of coastal garrisons was important. One significant construction at Pendennis was a new guard barracks just inside the Elizabethan entrance, which was given a pedimented façade, perhaps inspired by the Continental buildings of the great military engineer, Sébastien le Prestre de Vauban. The barracks and gate, built in about 1700, were a significant addition at a time when it was more usual for soldiers to lodge at local inns and houses.

A Prospect of St. MAW'S CASTLE

COLONEL LILLY'S MODERNIZATION

In 1700 France was still pursuing aggressive political and economic policies against England and other European nations. War broke out in 1702, with England in a European alliance to break French dominance. It was waged on European soil until 1713, with John Churchill, first duke of Marlborough, conducting brilliant campaigns during which English arms earned a fearsome reputation. Among major victories was that at Blenheim in 1704. In the first year of peace, 1714, Marlborough ordered a review of coastal defences, placing Colonel Christian Lilly in charge of the south-west. His reports for Pendennis and St Mawes were uncompromising. Whereas he judged St Mawes satisfactory, Lilly regarded Pendennis as 'in a very precarious condition, its garrison consisting but one company of invalids'. And further that 'the body of the fort having been for many years neglected is now in a very ruinous condition'.

It is likely that Lilly's recommendations of 1715 were not substantially implemented until the years between 1732 to 1739. At this time, the parapet of the Elizabethan rampart was reformed and many of the 85 old guns (of Tudor date) were replaced with modern ones both in the main fortress (for instance, Nine-Gun Battery on the east curtain today), and outside on Pendennis Point, in what became known as the Blockhouse Long Platform and at Crab Quay. The interior of Pendennis was stripped of its old barracks, windmill and storehouse, and a new storehouse, powder magazine, and gunners' barracks were built. The heaviest guns, 18-pounders, were on the waterside defences, answered by 17 guns mostly on the sea battery outside the Henrician fort at St Mawes, including six powerful 24-pounders with an extreme range of 1½ miles. Clearly, the main concern was still Carrick Roads and these guns could sink any warships entering the river mouth.

THE AMERICAN WAR

The war which led to American independence (1775–83) was not fought wholly on American soil. By this date Britain was the dominant world power. With her resources severely stretched, other European nations sided with the Americans to achieve their own political and economic advantages – notably France, Spain and Holland – and the conflict became international. In Britain extensive preparations were made against invasion,

Top: The north-east view of Pendennis, by Nathaniel and Samuel Buck, 1734. The waterside defences from Pendennis Point to Crab Quay are shown clearly

Above: Ethan Allen, American revolutionary imprisoned at Pendennis in 1775. He wrote in his autobiography, 'My personal treatment by Lieutenant Hamilton, who commanded the castle, was very generous. He sent me every day a fine breakfast and dinner from his own table, and a bottle of good wine.'

Above: Captain Philip Melvill (1762–1811), Governor of Pendennis Castle from 1797 until his death. He fought in India against Hyder Ali and Tippoo Sultan, was wounded, captured and imprisoned in Bangalore for four years. The experience may have led to the extremes of emotion he is reported to have shown

Below: Pendennis Castle with the Pendennis Artillery Volunteers, by Charles Tomkins, c.1800

including, from 1775, calling up the part-time militia forces at Pendennis and St Mawes, which remained until 1780. In August 1779 a French invasion fleet was sighted off Land's End and a force of 2,000 tin miners reinforced Pendennis; only the timidity of the French commander and adverse weather prevented a landing. New barracks were built at Pendennis in 1779 alongside the north-west curtain, cut into the ground for protection, and the gun batteries were maintained to deny Carrick Roads to hostile shipping. By the 1780s the sea battery at St Mawes had become a formidable armament of more than 30 heavy guns.

THE NAPOLEONIC WARS

The French Revolution of 1789 and the rise of Napoleon Bonaparte led to war across Europe as France pursued an imperialist agenda and crushed many European armies. Britain entered the conflict in 1793, when there was another review of coastal defences. In 1796 Colonel Elias Durnford, the Commanding Royal Engineer for the Western District, and Lieutenant Richard Fletcher, began extensive improvements to Falmouth's defences. Four raised gun batteries (cavaliers) were made to cover the landward approach at Pendennis, and a palisade and secondary ditch were made in the main ditch. The old outworks on Hornwork Common were levelled and the battery at

Blockhouse Long Platform on the waterside defences was abandoned. It was replaced in 1793 by Half-Moon Battery just outside the Elizabethan fortress. This had a better command of the sea and complemented another new battery across the estuary at St Anthony Head, about a mile south-east of St Mawes. At the height of the war, Pendennis was defended by 22 24-pounder cannon, 14 18-pounders and 12 carronades.

As war continued, the port of Falmouth became increasingly busy and by 1813 Pendennis and Plymouth together formed the main supply depot for the British Army. Britain was at war in Spain, fighting against Napoleon's armies, which had taken over the country and installed a pro-French government. At this time mail packet ships were armed with cannon and to prevent accident or sabotage in port they unloaded gunpowder at Crab Quay, storing it in the old blockhouse on the waterside defences, which was adapted as a temporary magazine.

Changes at Pendennis included a host of buildings for troops and storage, including temporary hut barracks built between 1803 and 1804 and a hospital on Hornwork Common. A fifth cavalier was added in the south bastion, with a magazine behind it, and Colonel Lilly's store building was enlarged and another one built (now the shop).

DECLINE AND REARMAMENT (1815–80)

The duke of Wellington's great victory over Napoleon at Waterloo in 1815 broke the power of France in Europe and brought to an end 22 years of war. Afterwards, Britain witnessed a huge reduction in the Army and many coastal forts were run down. At Pendennis many temporary buildings were removed and the palisades left to rot. By 1830 the hospital on Hornwork Common was ruinous, while soldiers' kitchen gardens and sheds, allowed towards the end of the war, had multiplied around it. Order returned only slowly, in response to renewed French military build-up in the 1840s. By the late 1850s, England and France were rivals in a race for military advantage, particularly at sea with steam-powered, ironclad warships, immune to conventional guns, equipped with new rifled guns that were more accurate and more devastating.

In 1852 Falmouth was considered unfit to face such challenges, with many of the guns at Pendennis and St Mawes now unserviceable. Rearmament did not involve any radical redesign at Pendennis, but more powerful guns were installed from 1854, comprising 19 32- and 56-pounders in the bastions at Half-Moon Battery and at Crab Quay.

At St Mawes, however, the Grand Sea Battery was totally reconstructed for 10-inch and 8-inch shell guns and a new magazine was built into a rock-cut terrace in the hillside. The Henrician fort served as barracks and the roof was given a concrete bomb-proof cover.

By 1859, 44 years of neglect had taken its toll on coastal defences; they were simply inadequate in the light of developments in warfare and the renewed naval and military power of France. In that year, a Royal Commission on the Defences of the United Kingdom began a nationwide survey which recommended drastic action when it reported in 1860. This resulted in a massive programme of fortress building in the 1860s and 1870s. Falmouth was largely bypassed, though it received powerful rifled guns in the 1870s.

THE RESPONSE TO MODERN WARFARE (1887–1914)

The period from 1880 to 1900, which was one of revolutionary change in the technology of warfare, most affected the Falmouth defences. Steel made it possible to make lighter, stronger guns; smokeless and more powerful explosives were developed and new weapons became widespread – the rapid-fire magazine rifle, submarine mines, the highly destructive machine gun, the silent, unseen torpedo and the fast, breech-loading gun. Other developments included accurate optical methods of range-finding, while telephones and electricity enabled efficient communication of commands

Left: Lieutenant-Colonel Burgess of the Pendennis Artillery Volunteers in about 1800, by Charles Tomkins. The volunteers were a part-time artillery unit set up by Governor Melvill during the French Revolutionary and Napoleonic wars
***Below:** Miners Militia officers camped outside Pendennis Castle in the second half of the 19th century*

Below: A late-19th-century photograph of Pendennis, showing what appears to be an exercise on the parade ground involving field guns and treatment of the 'wounded'

and target data, and powerful searchlights aided night firing.

Although a submarine electric minefield was laid across the entrance to Carrick Roads in 1885, with mines that could be detonated remotely by observers on shore (see facing page), it was not until 1887 that Falmouth was officially recognized as a valuable mercantile port, vulnerable to enemy attack, and requiring new defences. It was also important to the Royal Navy as the first and last port of call for ships in the Channel, and the Falmouth Docks Company, founded in 1868, included an important facility for ship repairs.

New breech-loading guns were recommended in 1888. Over the next 20 years Falmouth was designated as a Defended Port, with defences allotted to a standard specification and organized from a command centre at Pendennis. The new guns had several roles. Six-inch guns were to engage larger warships from new positions in One-Gun Battery and a rebuilt Half-Moon Battery at Pendennis, and at St Anthony Head. Quick-firing 12-pounder and 6-pounder guns were fitted at

East Bastion and Carrick Mount Bastion at Pendennis, at Crab Quay and at St Mawes, to fire on fast torpedo boats attempting to run the minefield. At Horse Pool Bastion at Pendennis, Crab Quay and St Mawes machine guns were installed for close defence.

A complex coastal fortress could not be operated by a handful of regular gunners supplemented by the part-time militia, as had been the case for the previous 350 years. It required a permanent staff. In 1902 new barracks were built at Pendennis to house the 105th Regiment Royal Garrison Artillery (RGA). This was a regular garrison of gunners, supported in wartime by the part-time soldiers of the Miners Artillery Militia (from 1908 part of the Territorial Force, which is itself now the Territorial Army). Many small buildings were established, including a War Signal Station on the roof of the Henrician gun tower at Pendennis, to control shipping entering and leaving the port, with range- and position-finding cells and searchlight emplacements on both sides of Carrick Roads.

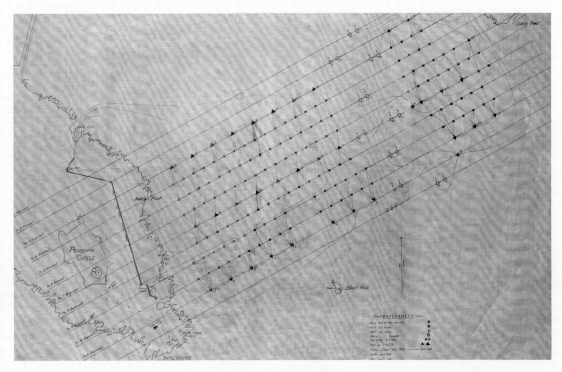

At Falmouth a submarine minefield was developed from 1885 when local men were trained as a volunteer corps of Submarine Miners

Victorian Ingenuity: The Submarine Minefield

In the late Victorian era the defences of important ports and anchorages became more elaborate. In addition to more powerful guns, lethal underwater weapons – explosive mines – were laid across harbour entrances to protect against hostile shipping.

Submarine mines were first used effectively during the Crimean War (1854–6). From 1871 sophisticated minefields were laid in British fortresses worldwide by special units of Royal Engineers, both regulars and volunteers. At Falmouth a minefield was developed from 1885 when local fishermen were trained as a volunteer corps of Submarine Miners. An HQ was established in 1892 on Bar Road opposite Arwenack House, and four years later a pier was made to load mines onto a mine-laying ship, the *General Elliott*. The Royal Navy took over responsibility for mining in 1907 and maintained it until the end of the Second World War.

Mines were circular or barrel-shaped metal containers holding typical charges of between 100lb and 500lb of high explosive (gun-cotton). They were laid from a ship in a network of known positions, either on the seabed (ground mines) or tethered at a given depth (electro-contact mines). Each mine was connected via an electric cable to a test room, located safely on shore. Observers in special observation cells at Pendennis and St Mawes could track a ship using a range-finding telescope passing over a chart, on which the positions of the mines were located with electric contacts. When the telescope aligned with the ship and passed over a contact, the mine could be detonated. An electro-contact mine worked when a vessel hit it, tripping an electric circuit through the cable to set off an alarm bell in the test room, where the crew could explode it immediately by a return signal on advice from the observer.

Above: A plan showing the layout and position of submarine mines and their connecting cables across Falmouth haven at the beginning of the 20th century
Below: Submarine miners at work with mines at a depot (unknown location) in 1904

A Soldier's Letters: Pendennis to the Western Front

John Glasson Thomas was stationed at Pendennis in 1916. His letters to his friend Gertie Brooks were found in an attic by Gertie's great-niece in 2002. On 3 October 1916 John was transferred to France. He survived the battle of the Somme but was killed during the battle of Ypres of 1917. Some of the letters are on display in the Royal Garrison Artillery Barracks, in the barrack room where John wrote them, as part of the exhibition 'Fortress Falmouth and the First World War'.

'If you don't hear soon from me in France, you'll know 'twill not be because I won't write.'

Above: Quartermaster John Glasson Thomas in France

Below: John Glasson Thomas sent this postcard to Gertie Brooks on 18 July 1917. Three weeks later, on 11 August 1917, he was killed in action on the Western Front

Pendennis Castle, 18 February 1916

Just now, it's blowing a hurricane, and promises to be a dirty night, but that doesn't matter to me, for I go to bed every night now, and really I'm having a delightful time. You can hardly fancy how strange I felt when first I was taken from battery duty. To have something definite to do every day, and to get to bed every night – well – I'm still thinking 'tis too good to last long … yesterday week the Dutch liner 'Rotterdam' put into Falmouth. In the evening, in torrential rain, I, with twenty others were marched to the docks, having our rifles, bayonets and twenty rounds of ammunition. Naturally we were in high glee expecting some important business. When we got to the extreme end of the docks, we were kept standing until we were properly wet through, and then were marched back to the Castle again … fifty of our fellows, together with fifty blue jackets searched her high and low for Lincoln, the ex-MP and spy, with what result we do not know, but the liner did not leave until Tuesday.

Pendennis Castle, 15 March 1916

I had a really interesting time last week, for we were doing some practical artillery work – firing. The weather was rather against accurate shooting for we had a strong cutting east wind, and the targets were often lost in the trough in the waves.

Pendennis Castle, 18 May 1916

2.15am – a fog as thick as a bag! St Anthony lighthouse is only 2,400 yards from our battery, but we cannot see its light, though we can hear the fog bell ringing. It is impossible to see far beyond the muzzle of the gun, and save for the thumping of the engines that work our searchlights, and the tolling of the fog bell everything is very still and quiet.

Pendennis Castle, 18 May 1916

It is now 3.15am and as dark as a winter night. I've just posted the new sentry and one can hardly see the length of the gun … All sorts of wild rumours re German raiders have been floating about, but this I *know* – although the newspapers have said nothing about it – that during the Easter weekend, six ships were sunk in this vicinity … Every night now we have five rounds of lyddite on the gun platforms, so you see we are in for business if anything comes along …

The day passed along very well, until, after tea, and then the fellows began to get fidgety at being 'cooped up' on a fine Bank Holiday. I spent my evening in endeavouring to take them away from themselves, by organising a tug of war between the gun crews, skipping contests, kicking a football and gymnastics on parallel bars. Strange 'goings on' for a Good Friday, eh?

Pendennis Castle, 3 June 1916

Here at my side now there is something which I'm sure you would very much like to have – a basin filled with a bunch of honeysuckle! Fancy! Flowers on the table in a battery shelter! … One of our fellows picked them within the bounds of our battery, and thought I'd like them, so here they are.

Pendennis Castle, 25 June 1916

If all goes well this is the last letter you'll get from me from the above address … The 173rd Siege Battery is in process of formation …

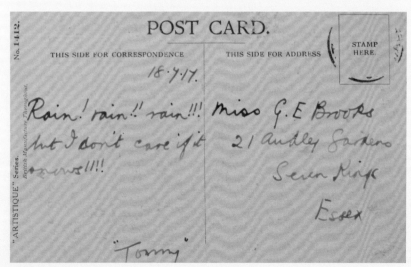

POST CARD.

THIS SIDE FOR CORRESPONDENCE / THIS SIDE FOR ADDRESS

STAMP HERE.

18·7·17.

Rain! rain!! rain!!! but I don't care if it snows!!!!

"Tommy"

Miss G. E Brooks
21 Audley Gardens
Seven Kings
Essex

No. 1412.

"ARTISTIQUE" Series. *British Manufacture Throughout.*

TWO WORLD WARS: 1914–18 AND 1939–45

At the outbreak of the First World War, Falmouth became the command centre for the coastal defences of West Cornwall from Land's End to St Austell, defending shipping in the Western Approaches and the vital entrance to the Channel. The defences were well prepared and the gunners – RGA and Territorials – manned the coastal batteries. Strongpoints and trench systems transformed Pendennis, St Mawes and St Anthony Head into defended areas. Thousands of troops came for training before going to war. As earlier in the Napoleonic Wars, Falmouth became a resupply port for the British Army, this time in France and Belgium. Royal Navy minesweepers used the anchorage as a base for clearing the shipping routes, while supply convoys mustered to embark under escort. The docks repaired ships. A floating boom was established between St Anthony Head and the Helford River to block the river passage while airships and seaplanes were used to spot and bomb German submarines, whose strategy was to starve the army of supplies by sinking the convoys. A submarine was sunk off Falmouth in September 1915.

The war ended in 1918 with no major attacks having occurred. Until 1939, Pendennis maintained a small permanent staff to train visiting gunners,

Above: Soldiers and sailors in a tented canteen set up on Hornwork Common above Pendennis during the First World War
Below: St Mawes Castle, now equipped for visitors not war, looking across the Fal to Pendennis

while St Anthony was dismantled and St Mawes hardly used.

When war broke out again in 1939, Falmouth had no heavy guns for its protection. A plan was rapidly implemented, with a headquarters controlling Falmouth's coastal defences in Pendennis Castle. Pendennis, St Mawes and St Anthony Head were rearmed and once more became defended localities, manned by the Home Guard. After Dunkirk in 1940, Falmouth was part of the front line of defences along the south coast. The importance of the port resulted in booms laid across Carrick Roads to prevent infiltration by submarines, while anti-aircraft guns and a network of tethered balloons (whose cables were a hazard to flying) challenged enemy aircraft. At Pendennis and St Mawes the threat from marauding torpedo boats was countered by twin 6-pounder guns – a devastating weapon that could spit out 120 shells a minute in a hail of fire. Longer range defence against ships at sea was provided at Half-Moon Battery and a reopened St Anthony. Both were provided with new covered emplacements to protect their guns and crews against strafing by aircraft. In 1943 both received the most up-to-date 6-inch mark 24 guns, eventually under radar control.

At all sites, numerous huts and temporary buildings was erected. The Pendennis Fire

Command Post was enlarged, a new telephone exchange was installed and the Battery Plotting Room, from which the fire commander could control, direct and monitor all data on targets and command all the guns, was established.

For the most part the Royal Navy was extremely successful in countering any threat from German naval forces. The main problem was aerial bombing and the main target was the docks. Several heavy raids on Falmouth took place in 1940 and 1941, and again in 1944, and in all cases some damage and casualties were sustained – including ships sunk and important oil tanks at Swanpool set alight. The Falmouth coastal batteries saw less action, though they opened fire on several occasions at E-boats (fast, light torpedo gunboats) far out at sea, notably in 1944 during the build-up for D-Day. At this time, Falmouth was a busy port as American troops disembarked for training before the great invasion of the Normandy beaches.

After the war the Falmouth batteries continued in use for training until 1956. The Coast Artillery Branch of the Army was then disbanded as guided rockets had replaced guns in the defensive role. Since then the great fortresses of Pendennis and St Mawes have been cared for by the State as sites of exceptional historical importance.